The Library of
Political Assassinations

The Assassination of
Medgar Evers

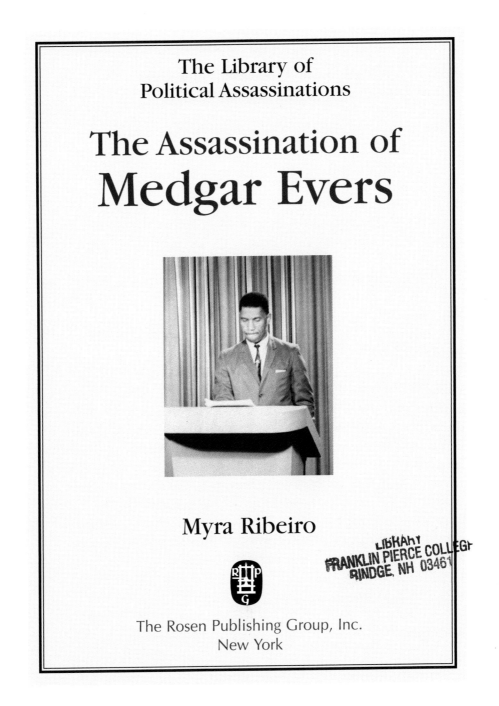

Myra Ribeiro

The Rosen Publishing Group, Inc.
New York

To Edi José

Published in 2002 by The Rosen Publishing Group, Inc.
29 East 21st Street, New York, NY 10010

Library of Congress Cataloging-in-Publication Data

Ribeiro, Myra.
The assassination of Medgar Evers / Myra Ribeiro.— 1st ed.
p. cm. — (The library of political assassinations)
Includes bibliographical references (p.   ) and index.
ISBN 0-8239-3544-2 (library binding)
1. Evers, Medgar Wiley, 1925–1963—Assassination—Juvenile literature. 2. Evers, Medgar Wiley, 1925–1963—Juvenile literature. 3. African American civil rights workers—Mississippi—Jackson—Biography—Juvenile literature. 4. Jackson (Miss.)—Biography—Juvenile literature. 5. Beckwith, Byron de la—Juvenile literature. 6. African Americans—Mississippi—Civil rights—History—20th century—Juvenile literature. 7. Mississippi—Race relations—Juvenile literature. 8. Mississippi—Politics and government—1951—Juvenile literature. I. Title. II. Series.
F349.J13 R53 2001
976.2'51063'092—dc21
                                                                2001002389

Manufactured in the United States of America

(Previous page) On May 20, 1963, Medgar Evers addressed the United States about race relations in a national television broadcast.

Contents

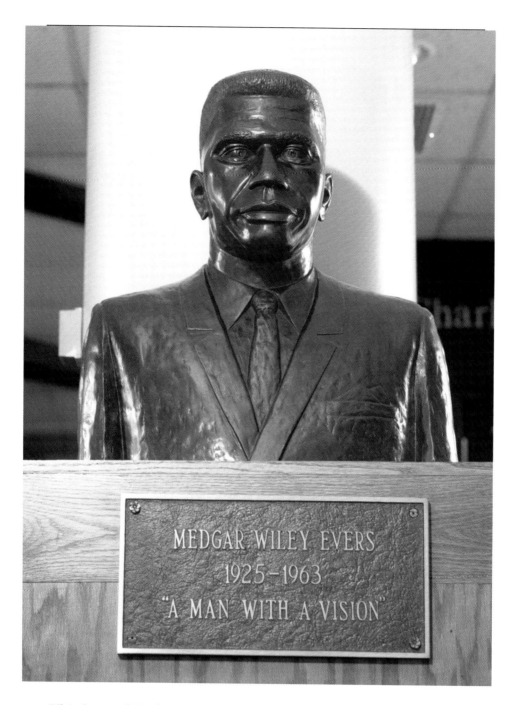

This bust of Medgar Evers is located at Medgar Evers College in Brooklyn, New York. The bust was made by Dr. Ed Wilson and was delivered to the college in the fall of 1989.

Introduction

When it comes to great American civil rights leaders, there are three names that immediately come to mind: Martin Luther King Jr., Malcolm X, and Medgar Evers. Although most Americans recognize the first two names right away, many people draw a blank on the name Medgar Evers. This is largely because Martin Luther King Jr. and Malcolm X were prominent religious leaders and national figures who created their own civil rights organizations and traveled throughout the country making passionate speeches for black rights. Meanwhile, Medgar Evers's fight for civil rights took place in the state of Mississippi.

Fed up with illegal racist segregation and the hate crimes against blacks that were the accepted norm in Mississippi at the time, in November 1954, Medgar Evers became the state field secretary for the National Association for the Advancement of Colored People (NAACP). The oldest civil rights group in the United States, the New York–based NAACP believed in non-violence and in arguing for black American rights in the courts. Their approach was to challenge and change unjust laws that discriminated against African Americans.

Before the civil rights movement, even drinking fountains were segregated in many parts of the United States.

Evers went to work trying to end segregation in Mississippi. Segregation occurs when a race, class, or ethnic group is not allowed access to the same places and services as the (usually white) society in power. In Mississippi, decades of slavery had resulted in a large black population. However, despite federal laws that had guaranteed their rights since the end of the Civil War, Mississippi's blacks were treated like second-class citizens.

Blacks had their own schools and their own neighborhoods and shopping districts. They were not allowed into libraries, movie theaters, restaurants, and public bathrooms. On public buses, they were forced to sit at the back. If a black man was walking along a sidewalk and a white woman was coming in his direction, the man would have to step into the gutter. If he so much as grazed the white woman while passing her, he risked being beaten or lynched by racist white citizens. In the eyes of the white policemen, judges, and juries, such a beating—even if it resulted in death—would be justified. After all, they argued, that black man should have known his rightful place.

Throughout the 1950s and early 1960s, Medgar Evers boldly challenged these injustices. At the time, the majority of blacks in Mississippi were poor and uneducated. They lived on white people's land and worked for white people. When Evers convinced blacks to register at polls and exercise their constitutional right to vote, these same blacks often found themselves jobless, with their houses burnt down and their loved ones beaten.

For years, Evers traveled around his birth state, talking to blacks and trying to give them the courage to challenge racist, white, Mississippi laws. Because Evers refused to back down, he became public enemy number one in the eyes of the ruling white supremacists. They believed that throughout Mississippi's history, segregation had worked just fine and that there was no reason for it to end. This was not just the view of a few extreme racists or Ku Klux Klan members (an association of hooded white supremacists who burnt crosses on the lawns of the blacks and Jews they hated). This was the view of the state government, the city governments, and the forces of law and order.

Over the years, Evers received many death threats. He was so concerned for his family's safety that he taught his wife, Myrlie, and his three small children to dive onto the floor to protect themselves from flying bullets. Evers knew the risks he ran by fighting to end segregation, but he took them anyway.

A Brutal Murder

Freedom has never been free ... I love my children and I love my wife with all my heart. And I would die, die gladly, if that would make a better life for them.

—Medgar Evers, June 7, 1963

It was just before 12:30 AM on the night of June 12, 1963, when Medgar Evers pulled his blue Oldsmobile into the driveway of his home in Jackson, Mississippi. It had been another long and tiring day, and to make things worse, a police car was following him. Earlier in the evening, Evers had called the FBI to report the incident and to give the license plate number of the car following him. The previous Saturday, an officer in a Jackson police car had fired shots at Evers and had almost run him over as he was crossing the street. As Evers jumped out of the way, he heard two police officers inside the car laughing at him.

It seemed as if Evers knew that he was a marked man. On that Wednesday, Evers had called his wife, Myrlie, three times to tell her that he loved her and to talk to his three children. Medgar and Myrlie had also discussed the day's big news: That afternoon in Alabama, Governor George Wallace, who had refused two black students the right to register at the University of Alabama, had finally backed down and allowed the students to register.

Myrlie was excited when she turned on the television at 7 PM to watch President John F. Kennedy give a speech. Inspired by the recent events in Alabama and other Southern cities, President Kennedy demanded not only changes in the law but also in "all our daily lives." He outlined a new civil rights bill, which would become the Civil Rights Act of 1965.

Myrlie knew that she was witnessing a historic moment. She couldn't wait for Medgar to get home so that they could celebrate together. As a special treat, she let the two eldest children, Darrell and Reena, wait up for their father. They sat watching a late night movie on television while Myrlie dozed in bed next to her youngest child, Van. When they heard their father's car pull up outside, the two eldest Evers children cried, "There's Daddy!"

The Fatal Shot

Outside, Evers parked behind his wife's station wagon. Little did he know that a man was crouched in the bushes 200 feet from the Evers's front door watching him through the scope of a rifle. Evers grabbed a pile of paperwork and some NAACP T-shirts from the front seat and slammed the car door shut.

A window with a bullet hole reflects the driveway and automobile where civil rights leader Medgar Evers was assassinated in front of his home.

Inside the house, Myrlie and the children heard the car door slam. Then, immediately after, there was another noise: the loud explosion of a shot being fired.

To the assassin, Evers's white shirt must have stood out like a white flag. The bullet hit Evers in the back, below his right shoulder blade. It ripped through his body, then tore through a living room window and a kitchen wall before bouncing off the refrigerator, smashing a coffee pot in the sink, and lodging itself in the kitchen counter.

As soon as they heard the shot ring out, Darrell and Reena pulled their baby brother onto the floor beside them. After a moment, they got up and followed their mother to the front door. Gazing out the door, they saw their father lying face down in the driveway with his house keys clenched in his fist. Blood was splattered all over the driveway. Hysterical, Myrlie started screaming. The children ran to their father and started crying, "Daddy! Get up!"

A bloody trail shows the path where Medgar Evers tried to crawl into his house after he was shot.

Final Moments

The Evers's next-door neighbors, Houston and Jean Wells, had heard the shot. They looked out their front window and saw Evers lying in a pool of blood. Reacting quickly, Houston grabbed his gun, stepped outside, and fired away in order to scare off lurking predators. He then went back inside and came out with a mattress. With the help of other neighbors who had come out of their homes after hearing gunfire, Wells lifted Evers onto the mattress. In the interim, a police car with two white police officers had arrived on the scene. The officers sat in their car and watched as Evers's black neighbors placed him in the station wagon and made their way to the University of Mississippi Hospital.

During the ride, Evers muttered and struggled to sit up. The last words he uttered were "Turn me loose."

As soon as he heard the news, Albert Britton, the Evers's family doctor, went to the hospital where Evers had been taken. He found Evers in the emergency room where doctors were trying to revive him. Dr. Britton felt that the doctors weren't working quickly enough. He wanted to help treat his friend, but this was a white man's hospital and Dr. Britton was black.

Medgar Evers's chest had been shot to pieces. Dr. Britton approached his friend and called out Evers's name. Evers turned his head and made a gulping noise. Then he died.

A Short but Heroic Life

It may sound funny, but I love the South. I don't choose to live anywhere else. There's land here, where a man can raise cattle, and I'm going to do it some day. There are lakes where a man can sink a hook and fight the bass. There is room here for my children to play and grow, and become good citizens—if the white man will let them ...

—Medgar Evers, November 1958

A Mississippi Boyhood

Medgar Wiley Evers was born in 1925 on the outskirts of Decatur, Mississippi. He had a younger sister, Ruth, with whom he was very close, and an older sister, Elizabeth. Medgar's mother, Jessie, was a religious woman who raised Medgar and his older brother, Charles, with a firm but loving hand. Medgar's father, James, who could neither read nor write, was a strong and fearless man who was proud of the house he had built and the land that he owned. Owning property was unusual at a time when most poor rural blacks were sharecroppers. Sharecroppers worked on white farmers' land and, instead of pay, were allowed to live on the land and have a small portion of the crops. In many ways, there was barely any difference between being a sharecropper and being a slave.

Lynchings were common throughout the United States before the civil rights era; white lynch mobs often terrorized black Americans.

As a boy, Medgar was quiet and studious, but he did have a mischievous streak. Every weekday, he and his brother, Charles, walked more than a mile to their school while the white children took the bus. When the white children's school bus drove by, the children would spit at the Evers brothers and throw rocks at them. The bus driver would purposely speed through puddles to shower the boys with mud.

Medgar's youth was filled with the injustices of racism and segregation. He knew victims of lynchings (his own father narrowly escaped being lynched), and every Christmas he saw white people throwing firecrackers at black shoppers in order to "see them dance." By his early teens, Medgar had developed a deep resentment of white Americans, which, by his late teens, had turned to hatred.

World War II

In eleventh grade, Medgar dropped out of high school to fight in World War II. In Europe, the company he fought with was made up only of black soldiers (the U.S. Army was segregated until after the war). All of their commanding officers were white. In Europe, Medgar was surprised to discover that white Europeans, unlike whites in his own country, treated him and other blacks as equals. He also observed the many similarities between Adolf Hitler's Nazi state and the white supremacist government that ruled Mississippi.

A Change Must Come

When Medgar Evers returned home from the war, he was determined to help put an end to the many racial injustices that existed in Mississippi. This feeling was heightened when, in 1946, Evers was prohibited from registering to vote. Soon after, he quit his construction job and finished high school. Then he studied business administration at Alcorn Agricultural and Mechanical College, the main state-supported college for blacks in Mississippi.

At college, Evers fell in love with a pretty seventeen-year-old named Myrlie Beasley. They met on Myrlie's first day of school in September 1950. A year later, on Christmas Eve, they were married.

The NAACP

After he graduated from college in 1952, Medgar and Myrlie Evers moved to Mound Bayou. Although poor, it was the only town in Mississippi that had been founded, settled, and was still governed by blacks. In Mound Bayou, Evers went to work at the Magnolia Mutual Life Insurance Company, one of the few firms in Mississippi that was owned by blacks. He also joined the local chapter of the NAACP. From then on, wherever he went selling insurance, Evers tried to get blacks from all over the Mississippi Delta region to join the NAACP. He also attempted to spread black pride.

At the time—late 1953—the University of Mississippi refused to admit black students. Because of this, at an NAACP meeting, Evers volunteered to try to desegregate the university by applying to its law school. In May 1954, in the landmark case of *Brown v. Board of Education*, the United States Supreme Court ruled that segregation in schools was illegal. However, despite this ruling, Evers's application to law school was rejected in September of 1954.

This setback only made Evers more determined. In November, Evers accepted the job of NAACP state field secretary for Mississippi. The position required that the entire Evers family move to Jackson, the state capital. Throughout the next nine years, Evers traveled all over Mississippi, working to get blacks to register to vote as well as to join the NAACP.

Emmett Till

When Emmett Till was fourteen
years old, he went to the tiny
town of Money, Mississippi, to
visit his uncle Mose Wright and
cousins. Before leaving Chicago,
his mother told him to watch out
for the whites in Mississippi.

This is an undated photo of
Emmett Till.

Three days after his arrival,
Emmett and his cousins were jok-
ing around on the porch of a grocery store when Emmett took a
picture of a white woman from his
wallet and bragged about having
made out with her. One of his cousins dared Emmett to go
into the grocery store and talk to the white woman behind
the counter. Accepting the dare, Emmett went in and asked
the young lady for a datc.

That night, two white men—the woman's husband, Rob
Bryant, and her brother, J. W. Milan—came to the house of
Emmett's uncle, where Emmett was staying. While his
uncle watched, the two men hauled Till away. Three days
later, the teen's body was found floating in the Tallahatchie
River. Part of his head was crushed and an eye was missing. A seventy-five-pound fan was fastened around his neck
with barbed wire, and there was a bullet in his skull.

Though the murderers had been identified and were
taken into custody, it took an all-white jury a little over an
hour to acquit them. Knowing that they couldn't be tried
twice for the same crime, the murderers were free to brag
about what they had done in an issue of *Look* magazine,
which was published soon after.

The Struggle Continues

Like many people, Evers was shocked by the murder and mutilation of young Emmett Till. The episode proved that whites could kill blacks for any reason they saw fit and get away with it. Evers's involvement with this investigation (and with the investigations of the murders of many other innocent blacks) had a two-pronged effect: It put him in the headlines, but it also made him many enemies. However, in spite of death threats and brutal harassment by the police, Evers refused to give up his struggle against segregation.

James Meredith

In the fall of 1960, Evers agreed to help a young man by the name of James Meredith enroll at the University of Mississippi. In spite of *Brown v. Board of Education*, the university was still not admitting black students. As a result of Evers's efforts, in 1962 a federal court ordered the university to accept Meredith. When the governor of Mississippi stood on the university steps and refused to let the black student inside, President John F. Kennedy sent armed troops to Mississippi to escort Meredith to his classes.

Police Brutality

In March 1961, when nine students from Tougaloo—a private college for blacks—sat down to read in a whites-only library, they were arrested and thrown in jail. The next day, sixty Jackson State University students protested the arrests in the first civil rights

Medgar Evers sits with James H. Meredith *(left)* in Jackson, Mississippi, as Meredith states that he will return to the University of Mississippi.

demonstration to take place in Jackson. The police responded with dogs, tear gas, and clubs. Two days later, the Tougaloo students were tried in court. When Medgar Evers showed up at the courthouse, he heard a policeman say, "There he is. We ought to kill him."

Soon after, while walking by a group of white spectators, Evers was hit in the back of the head with a pistol. Evers stumbled and almost fell. Two police officers arrived. "Get going, boy," they said to him. Then they clubbed him from behind. Although a white doctor examined him and (unsurprisingly) found no injuries, Evers filed a charge of police brutality. However, no charges were ever brought against the police.

Clyde Kennard

Clyde Kennard was a hardworking black man from rural Mississippi who had the same background, courage, and beliefs as Medgar Evers. The two men were also the same age. When Kennard's stepfather became ill, Kennard dropped out of the University of Chicago and returned home to take care of the family's farm. Though Kennard wanted to continue his studies, the closest college—the University of Southern Mississippi—was an all-white state school, and each of the three times that Kennard had tried to enroll, he had been turned down.

The day he received his last rejection letter, Kennard was arrested for reckless driving and for the illegal possession of whiskey. The fact that Kennard was a Baptist who never touched alcohol made it obvious that he was being set up. Nonetheless, he was convicted as guilty and fined. Shortly after, the bank foreclosed on his farm. Then Kennard was arrested on another false charge: A known thief claimed that Kennard had hired him to steal chicken feed. While the real thief was set free, Kennard was sentenced to seven years of hard labor in prison.

Soon after he arrived at the prison, Kennard began experiencing stomach pains. For months, nobody would treat his symptoms. Then it was found that Kennard had colon cancer. However, he was still sent to work in the fields.

Evers took Kennard's case, and as the two men became friends, Evers became obsessed with fighting the injustices committed against Kennard. As a result of Evers's efforts, Kennard's story was covered by the national press. The bad publicity embarrassed Mississippi's governor, who pardoned Kennard in the spring of 1963. A few months after he was freed, Clyde Kennard died. He was thirty-six years old.

The Civil Rights Movement Heats Up

By the early 1960s, the civil rights movement was heating up in the entire South, including Mississippi. As black freedom fighters became more organized, new national associations came to Mississippi. While the NAACP strove to fight racism in the courts, other groups, such as CORE (Congress of Racial Equality) and the SNCC (Student Nonviolent Coordinating Committee), wanted to take more direct action.

Greenwood

In 1962, the SNCC started a campaign in Mississippi to urge blacks to register to vote. In one county, the whites in power punished poor blacks by cutting off their federal food aid. In the town of Greenwood, many people began to starve. When the SNCC organized the delivery of food supplies, SNCC leaders were shot at and black citizens' houses were set on fire. In March 1963, Medgar Evers drove to Greenwood for a rally, where he made the following speech:

We're going to go back to Jackson and fight for freedom as you're fighting for it in Greenwood … When we get this unity, ladies and gentlemen, nothing can stop us.

The Jackson Movement

Back in Jackson, Evers and the NAACP began fighting on a new front. For months, the NAACP led boycotts of the white-run businesses on Capitol Street. The reason for this was that Jackson's main shopping district refused to employ blacks. Although time and time again, the peaceful protesters were hauled off to jail (often in garbage trucks), Evers refused to give up.

In May, Evers and two colleagues sent a letter to the mayor and the governor calling for an end to racial discrimination in Jackson's stores, parks, and public facilities. Jackson's mayor appeared on television and vowed never to negotiate. He told Jackson's blacks how "good" they already had it. Evers replied by reading a speech on television in which he announced:

> *The years of change are upon us ... History has reached a turning point, here and over the world.*

On May 28, some black students from Tougaloo College decided to sit down at the whites-only lunch counter at Woolworth's department store. Newspaper photographers and television cameras showed white customers pelting black women with food and garbage, while the men were beaten.

That evening, the mayor agreed to hire a few black policemen and crossing guards, but he refused to consider other forms of desegregation. Later that evening, someone threw a firebomb at Medgar Evers's garage.

Whites pour sugar, ketchup, and mustard onto the heads of sit-in demonstrators at a restaurant lunch counter in Jackson, Mississippi, on June 12, 1963.

On June 7, Evers spoke at a rally in Jackson. The speech Evers gave was one of the most emotional of his career:

Freedom has never been free ... I love my children and I love my wife with all my heart. And I would die, die gladly, if that would make a better life for them

Five days later, Medgar Evers was dead.

The Life of Medgar Evers

1925
Medgar Wiley Evers is born on July 2 in Decatur, Mississippi.

1951
Evers marries Myrlie Beasley on December 24.

Medgar and Myrlie later settle in Mound Bayou, where Medgar joins the local chapter of the NAACP.

1954
Evers applies to the University of Mississippi's law school and is rejected because he is black.

Evers becomes the NAACP's first state field secretary for Mississippi and the Evers family moves to Jackson.

1962
Evers and the NAACP organize a boycott of white businesses in Jackson that refuse to hire blacks.

May 1963
Evers signs a letter sent to the governor of Mississippi and the mayor of Jackson calling for an end to racial segregation in Jackson's parks, stores, public facilities, and schools.

June 9, 1963
Evers receives a call from an NAACP official who hears of a Klan hit list with Evers's name on it.

June 12, 1963
Evers is fatally shot in the back
with a rifle in his driveway.

June 15, 1963
5,000 people, chanting, "After
Medgar, no more fear," march
through the streets of Jackson
to pay their respects to the
late Evers.

June 23, 1963
The FBI arrests accused
murderer Byron De La Beckwith.

1964
In two separate murder trials,
in January and April, all-white
juries declare that there is
insufficient evidence against
Beckwith, who goes free.

1989
New evidence leads the Jackson
district attorney to reopen the
Evers murder case.

1994
On February 5, Byron De
La Beckwith is finally
convicted of the murder
of Medgar Evers
and is sentenced to life
imprisonment.

2001
Byron De La Beckwith dies at
University Medical Center in
Jackson, Mississippi.

A Man Named Beckwith

Byron De La Beckwith Jr. was born on November 9, 1920, in Sacramento, California. His father, Byron De La Beckwith Sr., had a prune farm that went belly-up after he drank and gambled himself into debt. Beckwith Sr. loved to hunt, and the house was filled with rifles, pistols, and knives. Beckwith's mother, Susie, came from one of Mississippi's oldest and most traditional families—a family that had owned plantations and many slaves, and that had fond memories of the "good old days."

"Delay"

When Beckwith was five, his father died from pneumonia, and young Beckwith and his mother returned to her hometown of Greenwood, Mississippi. "Little Delay," as his relatives called him, was fascinated by all the black people he saw in Mississippi. At that time, in California, it was rare to see blacks. In Mississippi, however, Beckwith's relatives taught him that whites were put on earth "to rule over the dusky races."

As a young boy, Beckwith enjoyed playing in the swamps where he would shoot birds and turtles with his .22-caliber rifle. He also spent a lot of time with his uncle Will, who loved to tell stories about the Civil War. All of Beckwith's male relatives had fought as Confederate soldiers. They were resentful of the North and of the federal government, and they glorified the pre–Civil War "Old" South.

Teenage Years

When Beckwith was twelve, his mother died of cancer, and he was sent to live with his uncle Will and two older cousins in an old, scary-looking house. At his public high school, Beckwith was considered friendly and funny but also as a bit of a screwball. Beckwith graduated from high school when he was twenty. He entered Mississippi State College but dropped out before completing his first semester because his grades were poor.

Shortly after Beckwith left college, Japan bombed Pearl Harbor, leading the United States to enter into World War II. Beckwith eagerly joined the marines and was sent off to the Pacific, where he fought in one of the bloodiest battles in Marine Corps history: the Battle of Tarawa. He came home from the war with a Purple Heart medal and a wife, Willie, whose drinking and swearing did little to impress Beckwith's respectable family. He also came home bitter and angry.

Brown v. Board of Education

Brown v. Board of Education of Topeka, Kansas is one of the most famous Supreme Court cases in history. On Monday, May 17, 1954, the U.S. Supreme Court decided that having separate schools for black and white students was unfair and unconstitutional. The Supreme Court gave the segregated Southern states until October to integrate their public schools.

Meanwhile, across the South, the decision created much outrage. The governor of South Carolina argued that it would lead to the "end of civilization in the South," while a Mississippi senator pointed out that "segregation promotes racial harmony." For many unhappy segregationists, the day was known as Black Monday.

As Mississippi was the most segregated state in the South, whites there were particularly angered by the decision. They vowed to resist integration. Thousands of white citizens joined the newly formed Citizens' Council, whose goal was to fight the NAACP. Basically, these councils were like the Ku Klux Klan. They controlled state and local government and businesses, and made sure that blacks were kept in their place. The state government itself formed the Sovereignty Commission, whose job was to keep the federal government from interfering with segregation.

Ultimately, *Brown v. Board of Education* created a hostile environment in Mississippi. Feeling threatened, Mississippi whites increased unfair and violent tactics against blacks who were beginning to claim their rights as American citizens. As the state's most active black organization and its most visible leader, the NAACP and Medgar Evers bore the brunt of whites' hatred.

Children at a newly desegregated grade school in Hoxie, Arkansas, wait to register for school. The famous case *Brown v. Board of Education* required the integration of schools throughout the United States.

Black Monday

A couple of weeks after *Brown v. Board of Education*, the leader of Mississippi's white resistance gave a speech in Greenwood, Mississippi. Judge Thomas Brady was a passionate white supremacist who felt that while whites had evolved into civilized, superior beings, "the Negroid man, like the modern lizard, evolved not." He said that because of their lower status, blacks should have been grateful to be slaves, and that they were no better than beasts of burden. Sitting in the audience, lapping up each word of this speech, was Byron De La Beckwith.

When Judge Brady published this speech as a book entitled *Black Monday*, Beckwith couldn't wait to sell copies. He also eagerly joined the Citizens' Council and tried to get a job with the segregationist Sovereignty Commission. At the time, Beckwith was working as a salesman for a tobacco company, and he drove around the Mississippi Delta selling cigarettes. However, as he explained in a 1956 letter to the Mississippi governor, Beckwith felt that his true talents could be best put to use by helping to "uncover plots by the NAACP to integrate our beloved State."

Beckwith wrote that, for him, the battle against integration was "a life or death struggle." He wrote "NOTHING ELSE IS MORE IMPORTANT AT THIS TIME! I . . . will tear the mask from the face of the NAACP and forever rid this fair land of the DISEASE OF INTEGRATION with which it is plagued with." He boasted that he had many skills for the job—among them, the fact that he was an "expert with a pistol, good with a rifle and fair with a shotgun, and RABID ON THE SUBJECT OF SEGREGATION!"

Birth of a Racist

After Black Monday, Beckwith became increasingly obsessed with keeping Mississippi segregated. In Greenwood, where he was considered weird but harmless, people who knew him—including his family—thought that his behavior and ideas were becoming more extreme. Beckwith would walk up and down the streets harassing strangers and preaching about the evils of integration. On Sundays, he stood outside the door of a local church with a pistol "in case any [blacks] tried to integrate the church." His radical views were even too extreme for some white racists. They were also too much for his wife Willie, who divorced him in 1962 after he had beaten her on numerous occasions. At the time, Beckwith was diagnosed by a psychiatrist as being a schizophrenic with paranoid tendencies.

Like his father, Beckwith loved guns, and he owned many. In 1959, an acquaintance, Thorn McIntyre, ordered an old Enfield rifle from a catalog. When Beckwith saw the gun, he pestered his friend until McIntyre finally gave in and gave it to him.

In May 1963, John W. Goza remembered Beckwith dropping by his tackle shop. He traded a gun for a Golden Hawk scope—a magnifier that fits on a rifle and is used to aim at faraway targets.

Leading Up to the Murder

In the days leading up to Medgar Evers's murder, there were numerous sightings of Byron De La Beckwith in Jackson. Several people thought that they had seen him sneaking around the rally at which Evers spoke on June 7. Around the same time, two cabdrivers remembered a white man asking them directions to Medgar Evers's house. The man said that he needed to find out where Evers lived in the next couple of days.

The weekend before the murder, the owners of a grocery store in the Evers's neighborhood had seen a well-dressed white man snooping around an empty lot that was for sale across the street from the Evers's house. The man drove a white Valiant with a long aerial in the back—the same car that Beckwith drove. He had caught their attention because he was wearing sunglasses at night. The owners' son remembered seeing the same car driving around the neighborhood on numerous occasions, including the night of Evers's murder.

On the night of the murder, two teenage waitresses who worked at Joe's Drive-In, the burger joint behind the vacant lot, remembered seeing a white Valiant with a long aerial in the parking lot. Although Beckwith later denied being there, there was no proof that he was at home in Greenwood as he claimed to have been.

Evidence

The day after the murder, Detective Sergeant Luke was one of several police officers searching for evidence around the crime scene. Following a trail that led to an overgrown field behind Joe's Drive-In, Luke saw something shiny sticking out of a

Jackson police captain Ralph Hargrove poses
with the .30-caliber rifle that was used to kill
Medgar Evers.

honeysuckle bush. Reaching into the brush, he
pulled out a 1918 Enfield rifle with a Golden
Hawk scope. One bullet had been fired from the
gun. Back at the police station, a full, fresh finger-
print was discovered on the scope. Before long, it
was discovered that the gun, the scope, and the fin-
gerprint all belonged to Byron De La Beckwith.

Justice Undone

*I come to you tonight with a broken heart. I am
left without my husband, and my children without
a father, but I am left with the strong determination to try to take up where he left off. And I come
to make a plea that all of you here and those who
are not here will, by his death, be able to draw
some of his strength, some of his courage, and
some of his determination to finish this fight.
Nothing can bring Medgar back, but the cause can
live on … We cannot let his death be in vain.*

—Myrlie Evers, June 12, 1963

A Nation in Shock

The day after Medgar Evers's death, Myrlie Evers spoke
these words at a Baptist church in Jackson. That same
day, a group of 200 students marched in protest through
the streets of Jackson. They were met by 100 policemen
who beat them, arrested most of them, and dragged
them off to stockades at a local fairground. More than
half of these students were under the age of seventeen.

Medgar Evers's assassination was talked about in newspapers, weekly magazines, and on television. The *New York Times* wrote, "Mr. Evers' martyrdom [has] advanced the prospect for strong Civil Rights legislation." President Kennedy claimed that he was "appalled by the barbarity of the act." Meanwhile, the local Jackson paper announced that "the most intensive manhunt in recent Jackson history" was searching for Evers's killer. Sadly, but unsurprisingly, Medgar Evers became more famous in death than he had been while alive.

A Hero's Funeral

Martin Luther King Jr. *(right)* stands with other mourners at Medgar Evers's funeral.

On Saturday, June 15, Medgar Evers's funeral was held in Jackson. Among the mourners was Martin Luther King Jr. The executive director of the NAACP, Roy Wilkin, made the final speech: If Medgar Evers "could live in Mississippi and not hate, so shall we. Medgar Evers was a symbol of our victory and of

Myrlie Evers and two of her children, Reena and Darrell, view the body of Medgar Evers at a funeral home in Jackson, Mississippi.

their defeat. The bullet that tore away his life four days ago, tore away at the system and helped to signal its end."

Five thousand people marched through the streets of Jackson to say farewell to Medgar Evers. As they walked, they chanted, "After Medgar, no more fear!"

The Mourning Continues

After the funeral, the casket containing Evers's body was put on a train bound for Washington, D.C. As the train made its way through the South, crowds of mourners lined

People hold a prayer meeting in Meridian, Mississippi, on June 16, 1963, around the casket bearing the body of Medgar Evers. His body was driven from Jackson to Meridian and placed on a train for Washington, D.C., for burial in Arlington National Cemetery.

the tracks at every station to pay their respects. In Washington, 20,000 people gathered at Arlington National Cemetery. Congressmen and senators witnessed a full military burial, which is normally reserved for heroes. Afterward, Charles Evers (Medgar's older brother), Myrlie, and the children were invited to visit with President Kennedy at the White House.

The Arrest

Meanwhile, back in Jackson, the hunt for Evers's assassin was in full swing. It wasn't long before all trails led to Byron De La Beckwith. On Saturday, June 22, Beckwith was arrested and charged with the murder of Medgar Evers. Dressed like a Southern gentleman, he spent that night in the city jail.

Most Mississippians—both black and white—were very surprised that an arrest had been made; over the years, so many white men had killed blacks and had walked away free. Because of this, no one imagined that Beckwith would be put on trial—much less be convicted—for the murder of a black man.

Life in Jail

While awaiting his trial, Beckwith was treated like a king in his jail cell. Housewives brought him home-cooked meals, and the sheriff allowed him to keep a television set and his personal gun collection in his open cell. A well-known white supremacist friend named Red Hydrick dropped by and advised that Beckwith not confess to anything. "I've killed a hundred niggers and they haven't done anything to me yet," he said.

Byron De La Beckwith *(right)* confers with his attorney at the Jackson police station after his arrest on June 23, 1963, for the murder of Medgar Evers.

Shooting His Mouth Off

Apparently, Beckwith was very proud of having murdered Medgar Evers.

✪ In 1965, at a Klan meeting, Delmar Dennis, a KKK member who was spying for the FBI, heard Beckwith give a speech in which he encouraged the group to kill their enemies "from the President on down." He also admitted, "Killing that nigger gave me no more inner discomfort than our wives endure when they give birth to our children."

✪ In 1966, a young woman named Mary Ann Adams remembered having lunch with a friend, near where Beckwith was sitting. When the friend brought Beckwith over and introduced him to Mary Ann as "the man who shot Medgar Evers," Beckwith reached out to shake her hand.

✪ In 1967, Beckwith moved to Jackson and decided to run for lieutenant governor of Mississippi. One day, while campaigning, he ran into one of the detectives who had tried to convict him for the murder of Medgar Evers. Beckwith hoped the detective would vote for him since he "of all people knew that Byron De La Beckwith is a straight shooter!" In fact, "He's a Straight Shooter" became Beckwith's unofficial campaign slogan.

✪ In the late 1960s, a Greenwood woman named Peggy Morgan and her husband gave Beckwith a ride to a prison to visit a friend. On the way, he bragged that "he had killed Medgar Evers" and was prepared to kill again.

The problem was that none of these people came forward with their stories until Medgar Evers had been dead and buried for more than twenty-five years.

The First Trial

The first trial began in Jackson on January 27, 1964. The team of lawyers prosecuting Beckwith made a strong case against the defendant. The only problem was that—despite the evidence of the gun, the scope, the fingerprints, the various sightings of Beckwith near the crime scene, and Beckwith's history as a fanatic racist—no one could place him beyond a reasonable doubt at the scene of the crime or put the gun in his hands at the moment of the murder. Then there was the fact that the twelve jurors were all white men. Women weren't allowed to serve on state juries in

This sketch by a courtroom artist depicts Byron De La Beckwith holding the gun that was used to murder Medgar Evers.

Mississippi. Although black men were officially allowed, they were never chosen to do so.

After five days of testimony and eleven hours of jury deliberation, the outcome was a deadlock: six jurors believed that Beckwith was guilty, six believed that he was innocent, and none would change their minds. A mistrial was declared, which meant that another jury would have to be chosen and another trial would have to take place. Until then, Beckwith, who was so sure of his acquittal that he had written numerous letters to friends bragging about his liberation, was led back to his jail cell.

The Second Trial

The second trial took place in April. It was much quicker than the first trial. Once again, the twelve jurors were all white men. Once again, they refused to reach a unanimous verdict and a mistrial was declared. The prosecution could have called for another trial, but the lawyers decided that there was no point progressing without any new evidence that could further incriminate Beckwith.

Although Beckwith was released from jail on April 17, officially he was still an accused killer and could be brought back into court at any time. That night, in celebration of his release, members of the Ku Klux Klan burned crosses throughout the state of Mississippi. Soon after, Beckwith himself was officially sworn in as a member of a radical KKK sect known as the White Knights.

On the evening of April 17, 1964, Ku Klux Klan members celebrate the release of Beckwith from jail.

Beckwith and the KKK

During the following years, Beckwith became increasingly involved in KKK activities. He quit his job and went to work selling racist pamphlets and books for the White Knights. By the end of the 1960s, Jews had also become targets of KKK violence and terrorism. In September 1973, the Klan decided to get rid of Adolf Botnick, a Louisiana lawyer who was an important Jewish activist. They decided to plant a bomb in Botnick's house—and the person chosen to plant it was none other than Byron De La Beckwith.

Ultimately, an FBI spy discovered their plan and Beckwith was arrested with a bomb in his car on his way to Botnick's house. Put on trial in May 1975—an earlier trial had found inconclusive evidence—the jury (which included five black women) found Beckwith guilty of illegally transporting dynamite. Sentenced to the maximum sentence of five years in prison, Beckwith spent the next three years in the Louisiana State Penitentiary. He was released early for good behavior. While serving time, he remained in a solitary cell and never mixed with the other prisoners. It was thought that Medgar Evers's murderer wouldn't last long among the other inmates.

Thirty Years Later

By the late 1980s, many things had changed in Mississippi. The state boasted a black congressman and more than 600 black elected officials, which was more than in any other state. Close to all eligible black citizens, who made up 35 percent of Mississippi's population, were registered voters. Furthermore, surveys showed that over 80 percent of white people under the age of thirty supported integration. When Myrlie Evers made a visit to the state in 1989, she realized that Medgar would have been proud of the changes he had helped bring about.

While things were changing in the late 1980s and early 1990s, there was much looking back to the days of the civil rights movement. Many lost documents pertaining to the Sovereignty Commission were uncovered. And many cases of unpunished violence against innocent blacks were brought to light. Before long, the names "Medgar Evers" and "Byron De La Beckwith" were front-page news again, and some people were calling for the reopening of the case. How could Mississippi ever go forward if it didn't address the crimes of its past?

Medgar Evers's Legacy

Medgar Evers's brother, Charles, became the first black mayor in the history of Mississippi.

The night Medgar Evers was killed, President Kennedy had promised the nation a new civil rights bill that would ensure equality for all Americans before the law. Two years later, following the assassination of Kennedy himself, this bill became the Civil Rights Act of 1965.

In Mississippi in particular, Evers's fight was not in vain. Ten years after his death, Mississippi had 145 black elected officials, and blacks were enrolled at all of the state's public and private colleges and universities. Also, more than one-quarter of black students in state public schools attended integrated schools where more than 50 percent of the students were white.

Medgar's brother, Charles, continued to register voters in Mississippi, and in 1969, he ran for mayor of the city of Fayette. When he won, he became the first black mayor in the state's history. Evers's widow, Myrlie, continued her husband's work at the NAACP. In 1995, she was elected chairman of the national board of directors of the association. Even in death, Medgar Evers's spirit continued to inspire others to fight for justice and equality.

Reopening the Case

After much deliberation, Jackson's district attorney, Ed Peters, decided that it was time to reopen the case. He talked to Myrlie Evers-Williams, who was living in Oregon with her second husband, Walter Williams. She was thrilled but cautious. Myrlie had wanted another trial for a long time, but she wanted to go forward with it only if new evidence was found. To help dig up new evidence, Peters put his assistant D.A. Bobby DeLaughter in charge of the case. DeLaughter set to work to find new evidence. He also had to track down old evidence because much of it—the murder weapon, the autopsy report, the trial transcripts— had disappeared over the course of thirty years.

Where justice is never fulfilled, that wound will never be cleansed ... Is it ever too late to do the right thing? I sincerely hope and pray that it's not.

—Bobby DeLaughter, February 4, 1994

Months of hard work and a bit of luck yielded promising results. The Enfield rifle that had killed Medgar Evers was found (by strange coincidence) in the closet of Bobby DeLaughter's father-in-law. He had just died, and DeLaughter found the gun while going through his father's effects. Some negatives of lost crime scene photos were discovered, and Myrlie Evers had hung onto a copy of the transcripts of the first trial. Key witnesses, such as Delmar Dennis, Mary Ann Adams, and Peggy Morgan, were discovered or came forward and agreed to testify against Beckwith.

An unrepentant Byron De La Beckwith *(center)* walks with his wife, Thelma, and his attorney. His attorney appealed Beckwith's conviction on the grounds that he was not given a speedy trial and could not adequately defend himself thirty-one years after the June 12, 1963, slaying of Medgar Evers.

One Last Obstacle

Once all the evidence was gathered and the new witnesses had agreed to testify, Bobby DeLaughter knew he had a good case. The only problem was that Beckwith's lawyers argued that trying their client for a crime that was committed thirty years ago was unconstitutional. They cited the Sixth Amendment of the Bill of Rights, which states that every citizen has the right to a "speedy" trial. A three-decade delay, they agreed, was hardly speedy.

Father and Son

One of the biggest obstacles to reopening the case against Beckwith was the missing autopsy report. Myrlie Evers agreed to let DeLaughter exhume her husband's buried body, but she couldn't face going to Washington, D.C. Instead, her youngest son, Van, made the trip.

When the coffin was opened, everyone in the room gasped. The body was perfectly preserved. Medgar Evers looked as if he were sleeping, not as if he had been dead for thirty years. Dr. Michael Baden, the top forensic expert in the country, who had reviewed the autopsies of both John F. Kennedy and Martin Luther King Jr., had never seen anything like it.

X rays discovered the fragments of a bullet still inside Medgar's chest. The fragments were large enough to be used for evidence.

For Van Evers, the moment was unforgettable. Since he had been only three when his father was shot, he had no memories of Medgar other than as a man who left bubble-gum cigars on his bunk bed. Now, suddenly, he was seeing his father for the first time.

The Final Trial

It took three years and legal arguments that went all the way to the U.S. Supreme Court before the trial against Beckwith was finally allowed to begin in January 1994. This time, the jury was made up of eight blacks and four whites. The courtroom was filled with Myrlie's family and supporters and NAACP leaders on one side, and skinheads and KKK supporters on the other side. On February 4, lawyers for both sides made their closing remarks, and on February 5, the jury reached a verdict. They had found the defendant "guilty as charged."

Medgar's son Darrell leapt up and shouted out a triumphant "Yes!" Out in the hallway, his shout was heard and the courthouse was filled with an excited buzz. Stunned, Byron De La Beckwith kept his chin up as the judge sentenced him to life imprisonment. Indeed, he would remain in prison until his death in January 2001, at the age of eighty.

When Myrlie Evers came out of the courtroom, she couldn't help raising her hands in the air and shouting, "Yea! Medgar! Yea!" She later explained her reaction to the crowds of reporters: "I had to jump in the air and shed some tears and raise my face and say, 'Medgar, I've gone the last mile of the way.'"

Myrlie Evers wipes away tears as she speaks to the media on February 5, 1994, at the Hinds County Courthouse in Jackson, Mississippi, after the trial of Byron De La Beckwith. She is surrounded by her son, Darrell Kenyatta Evers and daughter, Reena Evers-Everett. It took more than thirty years, but De La Beckwith was finally convicted of the murder of her husband, Medgar Evers. De La Beckwith was sentenced to life in prison.

Key Moments in the Civil Rights Movement

1954

In the landmark case of *Brown v. Board of Education*, the Supreme Court declares that segregation in schools goes against the Constitution.

1955

Seamstress Rosa Parks is arrested in Montgomery, Alabama, for refusing to give up her bus seat to a white man. Martin Luther King Jr. and other black leaders organize the Montgomery Bus Boycott, which causes the bus company to lose 65 percent of its income and costs Dr. King a $500 fine. Eight months later, the Supreme Court rules that bus segregation violates the Constitution.

1957

On September 3, nine black students are forbidden entry to Little Rock Central High School by the governor and the Arkansas National Guard. Three days later, a judge forces the governor to back down. When the students enter the school, they are harassed by a mob of 1,000 citizens. Finally, President Eisenhower sends federal troops to Little Rock, officially ending segregation.

1960

After he is refused service at a Woolworth's lunch counter in Greensboro, North Carolina, Joseph McNeill, a black student, returns the next day with three classmates. They sit at the counter and, again, are not served. When the *New York Times* focuses attention on the protest, black and white students across the country launch similar protests.

1961

Busloads of people lead a cross-country campaign known as the Freedom Rides to try to end the segregation of bus terminals. The nonviolent protesters are often violently attacked at bus stops.

1962

President Kennedy orders federal marshals to escort James Meredith, the first black student to enroll at the University of Mississippi, to campus. A riot breaks out and two students are killed.

1963

In Birmingham, Alabama, one of the most segregated cities in the South, blacks hold sit-ins at lunch counters where they are refused service, and kneel-ins on church steps where they are denied entrance. Hundreds of protesters are fined and jailed. When Martin Luther King Jr. leads a protest march, he is arrested and taken to prison.

1964

Congress passes the Civil Rights Act, which guarantees civil rights for all Americans, regardless of race.

The March on Washington that comes to symbolize the civil rights movement brings 200,000 marchers to the nation's capital. Here, Martin Luther King Jr. makes his famous "I Have a Dream" speech.

1965

A march from Selma to Montgomery, Alabama, to protest police brutality and demand the right to vote ends with demonstrators being chased and beaten by state troopers. "Bloody Sunday" receives national attention and sparks similar marches.

Congress passes the Voting Rights Act, which guarantees all Americans the right to vote, regardless of race.

1968

Martin Luther King is assassinated by a sniper at the Lorraine Motel in Memphis, Tennessee. He dies from a gunshot wound in the neck.

Malcolm X is shot and killed during a speech in the Audubon Ballroom in Harlem, New York.

Glossary

acquit To set free from an obligation or accusation.

autopsy Examination of a dead body to determine cause of death.

civil rights Rights of personal freedom guaranteed to United States citizens by the Constitution.

convicted To be found guilty.

deadlock Standstill caused by a tie between two opposing groups.

exhume To unearth a buried dead body.

forensic Applying scientific knowledge to a legal question.

incriminate To prove involvement in a crime.

integration Incorporation of different groups into society as equals.

lynched To be put to death by a mob.

paranoid Extremely fearful and suspicious.

schizophrenia Psychotic disorder characterized by disconnection from reality and fragmentation of one's personality.

scope Instrument used for viewing.

sect Group united by a belief or ideology.

segregation When a race, class, or ethnic group is not allowed access to the same places or services as the (usually white) society in power.

unanimous Being completely in agreement.

white supremacist Person who believes in the superiority of white people as a race.

For More Information

Associations

**National Association for the Advancement of Colored
   People (NAACP)**
4805 Mount Hope Drive
Baltimore, MD 21215
NAACP Information Hotline: (410) 521-4939
Web site: http://www.naacp.org

Web Sites

About.com—Civil Rights Movement
http://www.americanhistory.about.com/cs/civilrights/
   index.htm

The Mississippi Writers' Page: Medgar Evers
http://www.olemiss.edu/depts/english/
   ms-writers/dir/evers_medgar
Information about the life of Medgar Evers.

Videos

For Us, the Living: The Story of Medgar Evers. Directed by Michael Schultz. Television film based on the book by Myrlie B. Evers. PBS, *American Playhouse*, 1983.

Ghosts of Mississippi. Directed by Rob Reiner. Columbia Pictures/Castle Rock Entertainment, 1996.

Mississippi Burning. Directed by Alan Parker. Orion Pictures, 1988.

Southern Justice: The Murder of Medgar Evers. Ambrose Video, 1994. Originally broadcast on HBO as a segment of the *America Undercover* series.

For Further Reading

Brown, Jennie. *Medgar Evers*. Los Angeles, CA: Melrose Square Pub. Co., 1994.

Carson, Clayborn, ed. *A Call to Conscience: The Landmark Speeches of Dr. Martin Luther King, Jr*. New York: Warner Books, 2001.

Evers, Myrlie B., and William Peters. *For Us, the Living*. Jackson, MI: University Press of Mississippi, 1996.

Evers-Williams, Myrlie, and Melinda Blau. *Watch Me Fly: What I Learned on the Way to Becoming the Woman I Was Meant to Be*. New York: Little, Brown and Co., 1999.

Gregory, Dick. *Callus on My Soul: A Memoir*. Marietta, GA: Longstreet Press, 2000.

Massengill, Reed. *Portrait of a Racist: The Man Who Killed Medgar Evers*. New York: St. Martin's Press, 1994.

Morris, Willie. *The Ghosts of Medgar Evers: A Tale of Race, Murder, Mississippi, and Hollywood*. New York: Random House, 1998.

Nossiter, Adam. *Of Long Memory: Mississippi and the Murder of Medgar Evers*. Reading, MA: Addison-Wesley, 1994.

Scott, R. W. *Glory in Conflict: A Saga of Byron De La Beckwith*. Camden, AR: Camark Press, 1991.

Vollers, Maryanne. *Ghosts of Mississippi: The Murder of Medgar Evers, the Trials of Byron De La Beckwith, and the Haunting of the New South*. Boston, MA: Little, Brown and Co., 1995.

Articles

Evers, Medgar. "Why I Live in Mississippi." *Ebony*, November 1958, pp. 209–210. Reprinted in *Mississippi Writers: Reflections of Childhood and Youth*. Vol. II: Nonfiction. Ed. Dorothy Abbott. Center for the Study of Southern Culture Series. Jackson, MS: University Press of Mississippi, 1986.

Index

About the Author

Myra Ribeiro has a master's degree in history. Her specialty is nineteenth-century black history and culture. Aside from reading, she enjoys Pilates, driving her red race car, and tending to her collection of rare orchids.

Photo Credits

Cover © Hulton/Archive; pp. 1, 6, 14, 19, 39, 46 © Bettmann/Corbis; p. 4 by Cindy Reiman, courtesy of Medgar Evers College, the City University of New York; pp. 10, 35, 36 © Flip Schulke/Corbis; pp. 11, 17, 33, 37, 48, 51 © AP/Wide World Photos; p. 23 © AP/*Jackson Daily News*; p. 29 © Gordon Tenney/Timepix; p. 41 © Franklin McMahon/Corbis; p. 43 © Leif Skoogfors/Corbis.

Series Design and Layout

Les Kanturek